FINANCIAL FRUITION

A Guide to Help Grow Your Wealth

Shlomo Bar-Eli

Copyright © 2021 Shlomo Bar-Eli

Copyright: Financial Fruition: A Guide to Help Grow Your Wealth by Shlomo Bar-Eli
Published by Shlomo Bar-Eli
Copyright © 2021 Shlomo Bar-Eli

All rights reserved. No portion of this book may be reproduced in any form without permission from the publisher, except as permitted by U.S. copyright law.

For permissions contact: sbareli@yahoo.com, 657-291-1229

Cover by Lauren Stockner

❈ ❈ ❈

LEGAL

The content and information provided in this book are for educational purposes and do not substitute for legal advice from your attorney, accountant, or financial advisor. Effort has been made to ensure that the content and information in this book are accurate, however this is not an exhaustive book and no liability is assumed for losses or damages due to the information provided. You are responsible for you own choices, actions, and results.

CONTENTS

Title Page
Copyright
Legal
Introduction
Chapter One – Assets and Liabilities   1
Chapter Two – Revenues and Expenses   8
Chapter Three – Real Estate   19
Chapter Four – Income Generating Assets   26
Chapter Five – Leveraging   35
Chapter Six – Investments   43
Chapter Seven – Miscellaneous   49
Conclusion   53
About The Author   57

INTRODUCTION

The purpose of this book is to provide ordinary people with some insight into understanding and better managing their money. I, like you, am an ordinary person. I grew up in Brooklyn, NY. After receiving my degree in Accounting, I began working a routine 9–5 job and soon realized that it was not enough. I began investing in real estate as a second income shortly after restarting my career as a Physician's Assistant. Since then, I have been able to supplement my salary with several investment rental properties across the United States.

Beyond just working and making money, it is also important to properly manage your money. For example, if you make $100,000 a year, but spend $120,000 a year, you are worse off than someone who makes $60,000 a year but spends only $30,000 a year.

This book is a tool to help people make better financial decisions. I cannot guarantee you will become a millionaire; however, with a better understanding, you can use this book to improve your financial position.

One thing that is important to me is keeping it simple! So many books out there are too lengthy or wordy, and the reader loses interest before getting far enough into the book to benefit from it.

Aligned with that goal is another goal of mine — to help people who are not financially savvy understand these basic concepts and use them to better their lives. I remember when my sister had to study for her math test, I advised her that it may be true that not everyone can get a 90, but that does not mean she could not get a 65, despite "sucking at math." Even if you're not so great with numbers, these basic concepts are accessible enough to enhance your wealth.

Lastly, to achieve the goals above, this book will not be exhaustive. I will provide some basic information, but provide it simply, so that people can actually benefit from it, rather than providing hundreds of pages of unnecessary material.

Let's take a look!

※ ※ ※

CHAPTER ONE – ASSETS AND LIABILITIES

One of the most important concepts I have learned from taking accounting courses is Assets and Liabilities. This concept is so important that in every accounting textbook you will see the following equation (or a variation of it):

Assets – Liabilities = Equity

What this statement means is that if you take the value of whatever you have and subtract the value of all the things you owe, it will leave you with what you are worth.

It may seem obvious, but when you start looking at your daily financial activities with this in mind, it can help you make better financial decisions.

An **Asset** is something of value. It can be tangible or intangible, but as long as it can readily be converted to cash, it is an Asset. An example of an Asset is real estate (property). If I buy a house today, it is an Asset, because it is readily available to be converted to cash. The value we assign to it is the **Market Value**, which means that it is worth what people are willing to pay for it (this is usually based on supply and demand, but that is a topic that is better explored in an economics course). An **Expense** is something that has no value because it cannot be converted back to cash once purchased.

A **Liability** is something that you owe, or debt. For example, when someone buys a house, they may only have a portion of the funds, and need to borrow the rest from a bank. The bank will loan the money (and charge interest) to finance the home. The loan is a Liability because you owe this money to the bank.

A mortgage is an agreement between the borrower and the bank that allows the bank to secure the loan using the property as collateral. If the borrower fails to make their monthly mortgage payments, the bank can sell the home to recover the money owed.

Let's use the example of buying a house to show how Assets – Liabilities = Equity.

Suppose you buy a $100,000 home, and you pay for it entirely with your money. You do not have a mortgage on this property and therefore do not owe anyone any portion of this home. In this case your Assets (i.e., the home) = $100,000, your Liability = $0, and therefore your **Equity** = $100,000 ($100,000 – $0 = $100,000). Equity is worth.

The important lesson to be learned from this concept is that even though you spent cash, you still have something of value that can readily be converted back to cash.

❋ ❋ ❋

Now let us look at a similar example but change one of the conditions. Suppose you bought this home for a price of $100,000 but you only had $20,000 in cash and had to borrow $80,000 from the bank. In this example your Equity is $20,000. Why? Because what you have, (the home) is worth $100,000, you owe $80,000 to the bank, and therefore your Equity in the home is $20,000 ($100,000 – $80,000 = $20,000).

What is interesting to note is that, at this time, your Equity is equal to the cash put into the deal. Eventually, your Equity can change due to other factors like loan payoff or change in Market Value. We will discuss changes in Equity in more detail later.

Now that we understand what an Asset is, we should think about the things we spend money on: *Are these Assets?* Because if the things we buy are Assets, at least theoretically, we are not wasting our money… right?

The answer to that is *sometimes*. Now that I have laid some groundwork, let's take this to the next level.

Think about your Assets. Think about the things that you own and what they are worth. Are they worth more now than what you paid for them in the past? If the answer is yes, then you have an **Appreciating Asset**. Are your Assets worth less than what you paid for? Then you have a **Depreciating Asset**.

But wait! Above I stated that when you buy an asset such as a house, your Equity in it is equal to the cash you put into it. So how could there be a difference?

The answer is that the value of Assets changes over time. When you bought that house, it may have been worth $100,000. You put $20,000 into it and borrowed $80,000. But guess what? In a year, that house may be worth $120,000, yet you still only owe $80,000 (for simplicity, I did not include interest or loan pay down in this example). Now your Equity has increased to $40,000. This is an example of an Appreciating Asset. If you start thinking with these things in mind, you can purchase Assets that will grow in value over time.

Generally, real estate tends to appreciate in the long run (why this is the case is, again, a question of economics). We can generally assume that real estate tends to go up in value in the long run.

The classic example of a Depreciating Asset is a car. The second you purchase a car and use it, even just once, it loses a substantial portion of its value. Why is that the case? Because what determines its value is its ability to be converted to cash, and that in turn is determined by what people are willing to pay for it, which is typically less than what you paid when it was brand new. (This may not apply to collector's vehicles, where different factors drive its price up or down).

Before moving on to the next topic, there are a few things I want to point out:

The first one is that generally, when considering value and building wealth, the kind of Assets we want to buy are the ones that will increase our Equity (in other words, wealth).

The next thing I want to point out regards the first equation we looked at in the beginning of this chapter:

Assets – Liabilities = Equity

The above equation refers to a given point in time. Meaning, right now, if I took all my Assets and all my Liabilities, and calculated the difference, that would be my Equity. I can do this calculation at any point in time, and the results may vary because the value of these Assets and Liabilities may vary.

The last thing I want to mention before I close off this chapter — and this is key because this is what "rich people" do — is that some Assets can bring you Income. The next chapter is dedicated to **Income**, so we will get into some of the details there, but the takeaway is this:

If some Assets can bring me Income AND

I can live within the means of that Income AND

I use the remaining Income to
buy more Assets THEN

*I have a self-perpetuating flow of wealth which
will bring me financial independence.*

This statement is what motivates me to keep going. Let's take a look at the next chapter.

❊ ❊ ❊

Key Points:

Assets – Liabilities = Equity

This formula can be used at any point in time and calculates your worth at a specific point in time.

Assets have value because they can be converted to cash. Generally, the value assigned to an Asset is the Market Value.

Expenses have no value because they cannot be converted back to cash once spent.

Some Assets are appreciating, meaning their value goes up over time.

Some Assets are depreciating, meaning their value goes down over time.

If some Assets can bring me Income AND
I can live within the means of that Income AND
I use the remaining Income to buy more Assets
THEN
I have a self-perpetuating flow of wealth which will bring me financial independence.

CHAPTER TWO – REVENUES AND EXPENSES

In the first chapter we looked at Assets and Liabilities. This was important because I wanted us to understand how we should start looking at the things we purchase and think, *Is this an Asset? Will it someday be worth more than what I paid for it? Will it bring me wealth?*

Let's go back to the example from chapter one of buying a house. I mentioned buying a $100,000 house either with $100,000 cash or with $20,000 cash and borrowing the rest. It may be great that I used the money I had, or even used borrowed money, to buy an Asset. But how do I get money in the first place? How does someone get $20,000 or $100,000 to buy that Asset?

To answer to that, we need to understand two new concepts: **Revenues** and **Expenses**.

You can look at **Revenues** as money received,

or in other words, cash flow in. Revenues are sources of Income because when you generate Revenues you generate

cash flow. Expenses are costs, or money that you have to pay. In other words, Expenses are cash flow out. Note that there are sources of Revenue that may not necessarily produce cash immediately, but for the purposes of this book I will assume all sources of Revenue are in the form of cash because it will be less confusing and teach us the lessons we want to learn.

Another equation for us to learn is:

Revenues (over time) – **Expenses** (over time)

= **Income** (over time)

The key concept is that Revenues and Expenses are functions of time. You generate Income or incur Expenses over a given amount of time.

I am going to explain these concepts in a way that is probably different than what you are used to hearing; however, if you think of it this way, it will help you think outside the box and realize that time plays an important role when it comes to money.

Why is that important? Because this will help us conceptually differentiate Income and Expenses from Assets and Liabilities. It will also help us realize how we need to utilize our time effectively to make better financial decisions. Revenues and Expenses bring in or deduct cash over time, while Assets and Liabilities are a description of what we have or what we owe at a certain point in time.

Let's start breaking this down.

As we said earlier, you can look at Revenues as money received, or cash flow in. Revenues can be generated in many ways, such as wages earned or from the sales of goods.

Expenses are the things that cost money, or that have to be paid to others. Expenses are cash flow out. They reduce the increase in cash from our Revenues.

In business, Expenses are the cost of Revenues, but in everyday life we can look at Expenses as the things which we spend money on, and which will have no Market Value after their use. For instance, if I buy a banana and eat it, the money spent on the banana is gone. There is no money that can be made from the remains of the banana once it has been eaten. Its value is zero. I want you to think about this when you make a purchase: *Is what I am about to buy an Asset or an Expense?* Here are some examples:

If I have a job that pays me $20 an hour. If I work for 5 hours at a rate of $20 / hour, we can calculate that I earned:

$$5 \text{ hours} \times \$20 / \text{hour} = \$100$$

It is important to realize that this could only be calculated with time used as a factor.

Now let's look at a different example. Suppose I am a graphic designer. I charge $60 an hour, so the amount of cash I can generate depends on the number of hours I work. However, as a graphic designer, I also have some of my own Expenses. I may have to pay for a software subscription to do my work, and I may have to pay for commuting to work, because I work out of an office. The subscription costs me $200 a month, and I budget $50 a week for my commute (assume 4 weeks in a month). Therefore in one month, I know I will have $400 in Expenses.

I can do some basic math to calculate my break-even point — how many hours I need to work to break even? If I take $400 and divide it by my rate of $60 / hour, that tells me that I would need to work at least 6.67 hours (rounded up) just to break even.

Let's take it to the next level. We said Income and Expenses are functions of time. My software subscription fee is due for the entire month in advance, but my commuting fees are paid for one week at a time, at the start of the week.

We can look at our profit in a few ways. We can see that in week one, I need to work enough hours to cover my $250 in Expenses (4.17 hours), but in week two I would only need to work enough additional hours to cover the next $50 of Expenses that I would incur for that week (0.83 hours). If you continue this for the four weeks total, you can see that I would need to work 6.67 hours to break even (4.17 + 0.83 + 0.83 + 0.83).

The reason I went into such detail with this example is that I want to make one very important point: *When it comes to Revenues and Expenses, you have to pick a time frame for which you will make your calculation.*

In this example you can clearly see that looking at our Revenue and Expenses at different points in time can change the answer. We pick some arbitrary cutoff point at which we add up all our Revenues and all our Expenses and see if we were profitable.

❈ ❈ ❈

I am going to touch on taxes briefly, to show how everything we have discussed so far may apply to you in your everyday life. Most individuals file income taxes annually. The IRS is looking to see how much was earned over a period of time.

A very unpopular tax is a wealth tax, which taxes your Assets at a point in time, rather than a period of time. See below:

Point in time: Assets – Liabilities = Equity

Wealth tax would apply to this.

Period of time: Revenues - Expenses = Income

Income Tax would apply to this.

I often hear people complain that big corporations do not pay taxes. While this may seem frustrating to those of us who are not "rich," something to understand is that they will not pay taxes if they did not generate Income (i.e., their Revenues did not exceed their Expenses).

Tax avoidance is the practice of strategically using the tax code to legally reduce taxes. Tax evasion is illegal. This is the practice of lying to or misleading the IRS to not pay taxes that would otherwise be due. The "rich" use sophisticated methods to avoid paying taxes, but not necessarily to evade them (maybe some do...).

* * *

Now we can return to our example using the home purchase of $100,000. Suppose over the course of a year we do the following:

Earn Revenues of $45,000. Pay all our taxes and Expenses, such that we are left with $20,000 in savings.

Effectively our Income would look like this:

Revenues: $45,000

Subtract Expenses and Taxes: -$25,000

Net Income: $20,000

When we prepare this income statement at the end of the year, we can see that over the course of one year our Equity increased by $20,000. So we prepare our Equity Statement at this point in time:

Assets (in this case, cash savings): $20,000

Liabilities: -$0

=

Equity: $20,000

We can see that the Income from our income statement flows to our Equity Statement. If we wanted to calculate our change in Equity over the course of the year, we would do it as such:

Assets [beginning of year]: $0

Assets [end of year]: $20,000

Change in Assets: + $20,000

If we purchase the home using the $20,000 in cash that we have, we would still have some worth; however, our form of Asset would change. Instead of cash, we would now have property. Let's look at an example of this:

Cash [prior to home purchase]: $20,000
Cash [home purchase]: -$20,000

=

Cash at end of year: $0

At the same time, we would also have this following transaction:

Home: $100,000
Mortgage (a Liability): -$80,000
=
Equity: $20,000

✾ ✾ ✾

I want to show you one more example using these concepts. Suppose this same home that was purchased for $100,000, is put on sale two years later at a price of $140,000. How would this transaction look on our Income Statement and our Equity Statement? Let us assume the same mortgage balance for the sake of simplicity.

Income statement:

Revenue from sale of home: $140,000

Subtract mortgage balance due to lender: -$80,000

Subtract initial cash investment -$20,000

Net Income (on sale of home): $40,000

You can see that this sale generated $40,000. We can look at it another way and reach the same answer.

Income statement:

Revenue from sale of home: $140,000

Subtract cost of home: -100,000

Net Income (on sale of home): $40,000

Now let's look at our Equity Statement, assuming the transaction above took place. *This is at the time of purchase of the home:*

Home: $100,000

Mortgage (a Liability): -$80,000

Equity: $20,000

Because:

$100,000 – $80,000 = $20,000

However, now the home is worth more. And we need to prepare a new Equity Statement. Well, we know what the home is worth because we are about to sell it for $140,000. We know from above that the sale will increase our Income by $40,000. So we should be able to arrive at the same numbers when we prepare our new Equity Statement. Let's take a look:

Cash from sale of home: $140,000

Mortgage (a Liability): -$80,000

Subtract mortgage balance due to lender: -$80,000

Net cash: $60,000

Our Equity Statement would look like this:

$$\text{Assets} - \text{Liabilities} = \text{Equity}$$

$$\text{Or}$$

$$\$60{,}000 - \$0 = \$60{,}000$$

If you look at the previous Equity Statement we prepared prior to the sale of the home, you will see that we had $20,000 in Equity. Combine that with the Net Income from the sale of the home of $40,000 and you arrive at exactly $60,000.

❊ ❊ ❊

This may be confusing at first, but it is important to understand because it allows you to see how the passage of time can generate large returns, due to changes in Market Value and increasing prices over time.

I believe real estate is a great way to secure wealth. Even if you are not an active investor, you can take some simple steps to grow your wealth in the long run.

❊ ❊ ❊

Key Points:

Revenues and Expenses are functions of time.

Revenues (over time) − Expenses (over time) = Net Income (over time).

Revenues are sources of money, or in other words, cash flow in.

Expenses are costs, or in other words, cash flow out.

Income over a period of time will flow to Equity. The value of Equity in the beginning of the period will change by an amount equal to Income over the same period of time, such that the Equity in the end of the period will Equal the value of Equity in the beginning of the period plus the Income over that period.

Equity [beginning of period]
+
Income [over period]
=
Equity [end of period]

❋ ❋ ❋

CHAPTER THREE – REAL ESTATE

It's important that we spend one chapter discussing real estate.

At some point in their lives, most people will want to own a house or apartment. Even if you do not plan on becoming a real estate investor, it is likely that if you are reading this book, you are interested in developing a basic understanding of money and investing, and in turn want to avoid paying rent.

It was important for us to first learn about Assets, Liabilities, Revenues, and Expenses, because when dealing with real estate we come across all these concepts.

❊ ❊ ❊

Everybody needs a place to live. To have a place to live, you can either buy a property or use the rights to a property by paying rent.

Often owning a home comes with a monthly payment that is lower than what it would be if you were to rent, but again, you do have to obtain the funds for a down payment first.

So why is rent so bad? The reason is related to everything we discussed in Chapters One and Two. When you compare rent payments to monthly payments on an owned home you will find that the entire rent amount is an Expense. However, this is not the case for a monthly payment on a home that you own. Your monthly payment on an owned home generally has four components:

Principle

Interest

Taxes

Insurance

Lenders differ on who is responsible for remitting some of these components, like Taxes and Insurance, but ultimately, the money comes out of the homeowner's pocket. When you look at these components you will soon see that three of them are Expenses and one of them is an Asset. Let's define these terms.

Principle is the portion of your monthly payment that goes toward reducing your outstanding loan balance. When you pay toward principle, the amount of the outstanding loan decreases, which means that the amount you owe decreases. This will affect you in the following ways:

Cash will decrease

Asset (in the form of Equity) will increase

Liability (total loan obligation) will decrease

Even though you have cash flow out, you are still retaining wealth because you are getting Equity in your Asset. This is not the case with the other three components. Let's take a look:

Interest is the portion of your monthly payment that goes to your lender but does not reduce your principle. This is the fee that the lender is charging you to borrow money from them. Interest is an Expense. Interest does not return to you. This is cash flow out with no contribution to Equity.

Taxes are payments that you have to pay to the government for owning the property. This is another Expense because once you pay this money you will never see it again in the form of an Asset. This is cash flow out.

Lastly, we have **Insurance**. Insurance payments are paid to an insurance company to protect your home from a covered catastrophic event. Most lenders require that you have Insurance before they give you a loan. They want to make sure that if your house burns down, you have some way to get money back so that they do not lose the money they lent to you. This is also an Expense because every payment you make will reduce your cash and not provide you with Equity.

* * *

Now that we understand these components, we can compare monthly payments on an owned home to monthly payments on a rental.

Suppose you live an area where a rental costs $1,800 a month. At the same time, you have the funds for a down payment and can afford to buy a home that will cost you $1,800 a month in payments (Principal, Interest, Taxes, and Insurance).

In the first case you have to pay $1,800 every month in cash. Over the course of a year, you will have paid $21,600 in rent. In one year you will incur $21,600 in the form of rent Expense and have no Asset to show for it, since you do not own the property. In fact, you are likely paying someone else's monthly payments.

In the second case you still have to pay $1,800 every month, but you retain the Principle portion in the form of an Asset. From the $1,800 you may have a breakdown that looks like this:

Principle: $400

Interest: $800

Taxes: $400

Insurance: $200

As we explained earlier, Interest, Taxes, and Insurance are all Expenses. You do not get to recapture these in the form of an Asset. You might say, "What is the point?" Even after all this all you end up with is $400 in Equity.

That might be true, and it is frustrating but there are some other things to consider. First, $400 x 12 months is still $4,800 that you are, in a sense, paying yourself. Secondly, as a homeowner, you get to deduct your Interest payment on your tax return. While I do not want to get into the details of that (it should be further researched elsewhere or discussed with a lawyer or accountant), it is important to know that a renter gets no such benefit.

Lastly, the Principle and Interest portions of the payment, which in our case combine to equal $1,200 ($400 in Principle + $800 in Interest), are constantly changing. Assuming you have a fixed interest loan, meaning the interest rate does not change, your monthly payment for these two components will always add up to $1,200. However, the apportionment of the two factors changes every month.

To give a brief explanation, it is because Interest is front loaded. Every month a small portion of Principle is paid off your loan. And since your outstanding Principle balance decreases, your Interest charge decreases. Your payment is fixed in such a way that your total payment will remain at $1,200, but over time the portion of the payment that goes toward Principle increases (therefore your Assets and Equity increase) and your Interest expense decreases. If you want to investigate this further, I recommend researching "front loaded interest" and "loan amortization schedules." When you take out a mortgage, the bank provides you with a loan amortization schedule that breaks down the allocation of your loan payments for the entirety of the loan.

Another benefit of being a homeowner is that you have the potential to make money when you sell the home. If the home value goes up, you will end up getting more money than what you paid for the home. Additionally, some portion of the gains on the sale of your primary home is not taxable up to a certain amount. For example, if you made $200,000 on the sale of your primary residence, you will not have to pay Taxes on it (I recommend looking into this further by speaking to your accountant or researching tax law).

To summarize, we have learned from this chapter that for most people, it makes sense to buy a primary home instead of renting.

❋ ❋ ❋

Key Points:

With regards to your living situation, you can rent or you can make a homeowner's payment.

Rent is an Expense; you have no way to recover money paid as rent in the form of an Asset.

As a homeowner, your monthly payment will break down into:

> Principle
>
> Interest
>
> Taxes
>
> Insurance

When you make your homeowner's payment, the Principle portion of the payment is a payment to yourself, in the form of an Asset.

As a homeowner you can take advantage of tax benefits such as deducting mortgage interest.

As a homeowner you may be able to make money on the sale of the home if its value appreciates over time.

CHAPTER FOUR – INCOME GENERATING ASSETS

It is important that we spend one chapter on Income Generating Assets. As I mentioned, an investment in real estate is an investment in an Asset because real estate is something that has value and can be converted to cash. It also comes with some advantages:

It tends to increase in value over time.

Portions of the Exepense of obtaining real estate (aka Interest) are tax deductible.

In some situations, gains from the sale of real estate can be exempt from taxes.

These are all great characteristics of real estate if you own the home and are living in it. However, there is more to real estate. Real estate can also be used as an **Income Generating Asset**. That means that while real estate is an Asset that you can use in the ways described above, you can also use it to generate cash.

You can rent out real estate. In this manner, the property is leased to a tenant to generate cash. Tenants get a place to live, while paying you rent.

Let's look at the example from the previous chapter. We were discussing paying rent of $1,800 a month vs. owning a home with monthly payments of $1,800.

In the example of paying rent, the payer is the tenant, and the payee is the owner of the property. The owner is making money by leasing out their property. In the previous chapter we looked at it from the standpoint of someone who pays rent. In this chapter we will look at it from the perspective of the person who receives the rent.

The monthly payment is $1,800. From the $1,800, the breakdown looks like this:

Principle: $400

Interest: $800

Taxes: $400

Insurance: $200

For the purposes of this example, now as the

owner of this property, we will add a few small assumptions. Let's assume that the loan amount is $250,000. The amount of money that was borrowed from the bank was $250,000. Assuming a 4% fixed interest rate, 30-year loan, the monthly payment comes out to $1,194 (you can find mortgage calculators online). To keep it simple, let's round this to $1,200.

We also need to know our down payment amount to calculate our returns on this investment. Assume we put in $50,000 from our own pocket. This means the cost of the home was $300,000. We put in $50,000 ($50,000 of cash, turned into a value of $50,000 in Equity in our home), and the loan amount was $250,000. We can see that we put in 16.66% as a down payment ($50,000 / $300,000). Note that different lenders have different requirements as to the percentage that needs to be put toward the home to qualify for a loan.

We now have all the information we need to proceed. We know that if we rent this home out for $1,800 a month, we will break even every month on our payments. This can be calculated as follows:

Rent: $1,800

Subtract loan payment:

- $400 (Principle)

- $800 (Interest)

Subtract Taxes:

-$400

Subtract Insurance:

-$200

= $0

You can see from this example that the money you bring in every month by renting this property out will provide you with exactly enough money to pay all your bills.

What is the advantage here? Well, if you started thinking about this property as an Asset you would see that you are paying $400 to yourself every month in the form of Equity. Every month the Principle portion of your payment reduces the outstanding loan balance. This builds more Equity in your home.

After 30 years, assuming a tenant has been paying rent for this home, you would have an Asset that is worth $300,000 (and it will likely be worth more due to Asset appreciation). Your return over 30 years would be as follows:

$300,000 / $50,000 = 6 or 600%

Your $50,000 appreciated 600% over 30 years. Not bad! If the home doubled in value over the course of 30 years, your returns would be even greater. It is worth $600,000 and you invested $50,000. That means that in this case your return is calculated as follows:

$$\$600{,}000 / \$50{,}000 = 12 \text{ or } 1{,}200\%$$

❊ ❊ ❊

We have one more example to look at in this chapter which will give us another way to look at how we can use our money. In the example above I used $1,800 to be consistent with the previous chapter. Now I want to make a small change. Suppose this home can be rented for $2,000. To keep things simple, I will assume we have the same costs every month:

Principle: $400

Interest: $800

Taxes: $400

Insurance: $200

Therefore:

Rent: $2,000
Subtract loan payment:
-$400 (principle) and
-$800 (interest)

Subtract Taxes:
-$400
Subtract Insurance:
-$200
= $200 (or $2,400 per year)

This gives us a whole new way to make money. Not only will this initial cash investment one day be worth more by virtue of building Equity in our home, but we can also get cash today as a return! This is phenomenal.

How can we calculate our returns? There are two ways to look at it: Net Operating Income (NOI) and Cash on Cash Return.

NOI is calculated by taking Revenues from the property and subtracting Expenses (not including mortgage payments). This will tell you how profitable the property is but may not tell you if a property is cash flow positive or cash flow negative. This is because, as we saw above, a property may just break even, in which case you are not getting cash, but still be profitable in the sense that you are getting Equity in the form of the Asset (Principle pay down).

Cash on Cash return calculates how much cash comes in from the property compared to how much cash was put into the investment. You would take Revenues and subtract your Expenses and mortgage payments. This shows you how much cash you get after all your payments are made. I like this calculation better, because I can easily tell if a property is cash flow positive.

If a property is cash flow negative, it may still be worth buying. You have to ask yourself, *Is this worth paying a few dollars every month to end up with an Asset that is paid off by someone else?*

Let's use the example above to calculate Cash on Cash Return:

Rent: $2,000
Subtract loan payment:

-$400 (principle) and

-$800 (interest)

Subtract Taxes:

-$400

Subtract Insurance:

-$200

= $200 (or $2,400 per year)

Here you have a positive Cash on Cash Return. But to calculate the percentage return you will need to know how much cash you put into the property in the first place. Like we said earlier, we are assuming that you put in $50,000 as a down payment. In this case, your Cash on Cash Return is calculated as follows:

$2,400 / year
$50,000 =
4.8%

Everybody has different comfort levels and there is no single answer as to what is a good Cash on Cash Return. You can look at a variety of different investments and compare them.

Some people may opt for properties in riskier neighborhoods, where the Cash on Cash Return is higher, but run into trouble collecting rents or pay for more repairs due to the quality of tenant. Others may opt for a lower Cash on Cash Return and be comfortable with a small, steady Income flow that allows them to pay down their mortgage.

Key Points:

Real estate can be used as an Income Generating Asset.

The cash generated by real estate can be used to gain Equity, or if high enough, provide a positive cash return.

NOI is calculated by taking Revenues and subtracting Expenses (not including mortgage payments). This will tell you how profitable the property is but may not tell you if a property is cash flow positive or cash flow negative.

Cash on Cash Return tells us how much cash comes in from a property compared to how much cash was put into it as an investment.

A property that is cash flow negative may still be worth buying depending on your comfort level and how much cash you have to put in every month.

CHAPTER FIVE – LEVERAGING

It's important that we spend one chapter discussing **Leveraging**. As we saw earlier, we can purchase an Asset such as a property and rent it to generate cash. Let's bring back the same example we have been using:

Rent: $2,000

Subtract loan payment:

- $400 (principle) and

- $800 (interest)

Subtract Taxes:

- $400

Subtract Insurance:

- $200

= $200 (or $2,400 per year)

In this example, we can see how much cash we can potentially bring in every month or year. $200 a month or $2,400 a year is great, right? Well, it depends. If we had $1,000,000 bringing in $2,400 a year that would only be a 0.24% return. The return is relative to our investment. To calculate our percentage return, we need to know how much we put in to begin with.

Using the same property from the previous chapter, we will be able to highlight something significant. Recall that the home cost $300,000. If we used $300,000 from our savings to buy a property and then charged rent, what would our returns look like?

Rent: $2,000

Subtract Taxes:

- $400

Subtract Insurance:

- $200

= $1,400 (or $16,800)

Notice that I removed the Principle and Interest payment since we have no obligation to a bank. You might look at these figures and think they are way better than the numbers we saw earlier. *Not exactly.*

Even though we are getting more cash as an

absolute value, remember that we had to put in more cash in the first place. It may be great if we have that kind of money lying around, but not everyone does. Secondly, if we expressed this as a percentage, we might find that we are better off borrowing the money even if we have the funds available.

You can make $16,800 a year on this investment, but you had to put in $300,000. When you take $16,800 and divide it by $300,000, you see that you are earning a 5.6% return on your investment.

Now let's calculate the return for the same property but assume we are putting down $50,000. The home still costs $300,000, but now we need to factor in our monthly mortgage payment:

Rent: $2,000

Subtract loan payment:

- $400 (principle) and

- $800 (interest)

Subtract Taxes:

- $400

Subtract Insurance:

- $200

= $200 (or $2,400 per year)

As we have seen in the last chapter this equates to:

$$\frac{\$2,400 \text{ / year}}{\$50,000} = 4.8\%$$

This only comes out to 4.8%. When we paid all cash for the home, we got 5.6%. Why is it still less?

You may recall that to generate $16,800 a year (or 5.6%) we had to use up all of our $300,000. In the second example, we borrowed most of the funds. We generated $2,400 a year (or 4.8%) but we only used $50,000. We still have $250,000 left to use. So, what if we used the remaining funds to buy five more homes?

In this case we would own six homes with $50,000 of Equity and a loan balance of $250,000 on each. We can generate a $2,400 Cash on Cash Return on each home and we have six homes. This means we would generate $14,400 a year in cash, which is still 4.8% of $300,000. However, keep a few things in mind:

1. This is nearly as much as the $16,800 generated by one home.

2. We are getting at least $400 in Equity in each home, so we are getting an Asset value of $2,800 ($2,400 + $400) every year per home or $16,800 per year, similar to the returns generated

when paying all cash for the homes.

3. Over time the principle portion of the monthly payment will increase, so the Equity generated over time will be larger.

4. You will have more homes under your belt.

5. At the end of 30 years you will have six assets worth at least $300,000 each ($1,800,000 total) versus one Asset worth $300,000.

We can forego all of the above and make a simple calculation to prove our point:

If we had to use $50,000 to generate a 4.8% return, and we had to use $300,000 to generate a 5.6% return, then the additional increase in percentage return of 0.8% (which is a 16.67% increase [{5.6%-4.8%}/4.8%] cost us an additional 500% [{$300,000-$50,000}/$50,000].

※ ※ ※

Everything we have seen in this chapter points to one concept: **Leveraging**.

Leveraging is a multiplier. It allows you to multiply your returns on an investment by using the funding from the bank to help generate those returns. This allows you to put less money into a single investment thereby multiplying your returns.

Using our example above we can calculate the following:

Cost of home: $300,000

Initial investment: $50,000

Multiplier = $300,000 / $50,000 = 6

This means that the revenue produced by this Asset is six times greater than it would be if we had not borrowed the money. While realistically this is not true because a loan comes at a cost (i.e. Interest), we can theoretically see two things:

1. We could multiply our return by to 600% if Interest were 0%

2. As Interest approaches 0% our maximum return approaches our multiplier.

Plug in the numbers for yourself and you would see:

Rent: $2,000

Subtract Taxes:

- $400

Subtract Insurance:

-$200

= $1,400 (or $16,800 per year)

In the calculation above I assumed Interest was 0%. Do not worry about Principle pay down because it is actually Equity. That means that $16,800 / $50,000 = 33.6%.

Remember that $16,800 a year / $300,000 was a 5.6% return. If you multiply 5.6% by 6, guess what number you get?

The answer: 33.6%

So, as we have seen, Leveraging allows you to multiply your returns on your investments.

❋ ❋ ❋

Key Points:

Our return is always relative to our investment, or the amount we put in.

Leveraging allows you to multiply your returns on an investment by using the bank's funding to help generate returns. This allows you to put less money into a single investment thereby multiplying your returns.

Real estate is an Asset that can be leveraged to increase your returns.

CHAPTER SIX – INVESTMENTS

We have gotten through some of the more difficult money concepts. Now we will spend one chapter discussing investments in general.

As we have seen, real estate is a type of investment, but there are many other investments out there. This is not an all-encompassing guide to investments; it is just meant to provide you with an awareness of the options available out there to invest in.

Cash is the most liquid form of money, which means it is readily available to spend. Cash does not necessarily mean physically held money. It means you have a form of currency which is readily available to use as needed. This can be physical cash or dollars stored in the bank.

Stocks are another form of investment. Stocks are ownership rights to a company. If a company wants to raise capital or funding, they might sell stocks. Holders of the stocks receive rights to the profits of the company, while the company issuing the stocks raise capital. This can be beneficial to both parties.

For example, suppose a company wants to expand its services. They need large sums of money in order to do so. They issue stocks to raise the funding, which will (hopefully) in turn allow them to be more profitable. The shareholder hopes to share in the profit of the company. Here are some things to keep in mind about stocks:

1. They are less liquid than cash. This is because they are traded on an exchange. If you have a stock, and the market is closed because it is late at night, you cannot convert the stock to cash until the market opens. Therefore, it is less liquid than cash.

2. Stock prices can fluctuate greatly depending on many conditions. Some are related to the performance of the company and some are related to the overall market.

3. Profit from stocks can come from dividends or growth (increase in value) of the stock.

4. Some stocks offer a consistent dividend. This means the company pays money to the shareholder for every share they hold. Some people prefer this cash payout.

5. Others, prefer stocks that re-invest their profits into the company so they can further grow it.

Some investors prefer this form of investment because they believe the company's growth will outpace the profits they would have otherwise gotten via dividends.

Another type of investment is a bond. A bond is issued by a borrower when an investor lends them money. The issuer then pays the money back to the investor with Interest. The investor does not receive ownership in this case. Bonds can be issued by companies or by the government.

A Real Estate Investment Trust (REIT) is another type of investment where the company owns or manages Income producing real estate and distributes profits to investors. Think about when we discussed real estate investing, but on a large scale. A company buys thousands of properties which they rent out to generate profits, and they use the profits to further grow their business or pay dividends to shareholders.

Another type of investment is a mutual fund, where money from multiple investors is pooled together and the manager of the fund decides where to allocate the money. They can invest it in a variety of stocks, bonds, or other securities.

The last thing I want to mention is an index. An index is a performance indicator. That means that whatever the index tracks can be used as a benchmark to understand something. You may often hear that the "market" is tanking or the "market" is doing well. What does that mean? How can you measure "the market"? You can look at the performance of an index.

Three well-known indices are the Dow Jones Industrial Average (DJIA), the S&P 500, and the NASDAQ. The DJIA is comprised of 30 large companies that trade on the New York Stock Exchange. The S&P 500 includes 500 large publicly traded companies. The NASDAQ is more technology focused, and includes 3,000 different stocks.

Why are these indices so important? Historically, the returns generated by investing in these indices can be tracked. There are many different ways to invest, but as we saw earlier, these can be used as a benchmark. Many investors want to beat the returns generated by these indices, so they may invest in a mutual fund, which has a manager who allocates the money. Investor may also pick the individual stocks themselves.

Novice investors would benefit from investing in large indices like these because (although past performance is not a guarantee of future performance) they generally are stable and consistent. They also provide a mix of stocks. Buying into many different companies protects the investor in case one company fails or goes bankrupt.

It is important to note that all forms of investing come with risk. There is no guarantee that the values of these investments will go up. However, investors can diversify their portfolio to reduce risk. In a diverse portfolio, investments are allocated to a variety of different Assets. If the real estate sector is having a bad year and all of your investments are in real estate, you may experience a substantial loss that year. If only a quarter of your portfolio is invested in real estate, you would limit your loss in that period, as some of your other investments may have a better year than real estate.

Key Points:

Cash is the most liquid form of money.

There are a variety of different investments available to investors.

Different investments come with different risks, and past performance is never a guarantee of future performance.

Portfolio diversification helps reduce risk, by allocating money to a variety of different investments.

An index is a performance indicator. Whatever the index tracks can be used as a benchmark to measure something else.

Many indices are made of a variety of individual investments. Some investors see this as safer, while others prefer to invest in individual stocks or bonds.

CHAPTER SEVEN – MISCELLANEOUS

For this last chapter, I want to touch on a variety of things that can help you with your finances, even indirectly. The advice here may be more related to habit than particular financial moves that you can make.

I used to shop online every day. In one year alone, I made over 1,000 online purchases. Many of us know how easy it is to shop online. You just click and a few days or even a few hours later it comes to your door.

I am glad to say that I have managed to curb my online shopping, and I am happier for it. The reason is two-fold: I am saving money and I have less junk in my home.

At one point I came across a documentary about Minimalism, and while I do not consider myself a full-fledged Minimalist, employing this kind of outlook has helped me think about my daily purchases and ask myself if I really need them.

For a long time, I acquired many things — toys, gadgets, watches, etc. I think this is because, as an adult, I have access to more money and a steady paycheck. But recently my outlook has changed. I try to avoid buying unnecessary things, and instead try to accumulate experiences. I realized that if I do spend money, I enjoy spending it on experiences — travel, dining, going to museums. Stuff is just stuff, and it can be enjoyable, but sometimes if you forego these things you will be happier for it.

No one can have the same experience as you. They can share an experience with you, but yours is unique. *You, and only you, know how you feel about it.*

Another way I feed the shopping addiction is to shop for Assets. That may sound silly, but if you enjoy spending money, why not spend it on something that will one day bring you more money? If you spend it on Assets that will in turn provide you with more spending money one day.

This is a good time to re-iterate something I mentioned earlier:

If some Assets can bring me Income,

AND

I can live within the means of that Income,

AND

I use the remaining Income to buy more Assets,

THEN

I have a self-perpetuating flow of wealth which will bring me financial independence.

This is one of the most important takeaways from this book. Anyone can employ this mindset. The goal should be to reach a point where your monthly spending, including bills and recreation, is exceeded by the Income provided by your Assets. When you reach this point, you will be in control of your life.

As you begin your own journey and research, you will find references to financial freedom and passive income. This means freedom from a job or the need to work. It means if you had to leave your job tomorrow, you would not necessarily need another job to replace it. You can pay your bills and survive in the interim.

Unfortunately, many people are tied to their job. They have no choice and no say. If they want to survive, that have to work.

So how do people achieve financial freedom? By now you should know exactly what they do. They build a portfolio of Income Generating Assets. This is passive Income — where you are not necessarily "working," but you still have money coming in.

That is not to say real estate investing or investing in the stock market does not require any work. To be successful, one still has to research and stay up to date with the markets or trends. However, these are things that people can do anywhere, and they can do it themselves or with the help of others. The key is that they have no one to answer to. They are free from the oppression of work.

CONCLUSION

I hope this book has helped you start thinking differently about money and investing. While this book does not provide you with any single investing strategy, it highlights some key points about how to better manage money and change the way you think about spending and investing.

In the first chapter, we learned how to assess our financial status at a single point in time. We learned that:

Assets – Liabilities = Equity

This equation provided us with a quick way to determine our financial status at a point in time.

In the second chapter, we learned that we need a source of Income to build Equity. We learned that:

Revenues (over time) – Expenses (over time) = Net Income (over time)

We then learned that by calculating our Income over a period of time, we can see the change in Equity from the beginning of that period to the end of that period. Income over a period of time will flow to Equity. The value of Equity in the beginning of the period will change by an amount equal to Income over the same period of time, to equal to Equity at the end of that period.

In the third chapter, we discussed real estate. We learned that if you compare the rent expense of a property to the mortgage payment of a similar property, it usually makes more financial sense to be a property owner than a renter. We learned that as a homeowner, you build Equity in your home over time, and you get tax advantages that renters do not.

In the fourth chapter, we took a closer look at real estate. We learned that not only is it an Asset, but it can also be used as an Income Generating Asset.

In chapter five, we saw that by borrowing money from the bank, we can Leverage our investment. This means that we can multiply our returns at the cost of paying Interest to borrow the money.

In chapter six, we learned about other investments that we might allocate some of our money to. We learned that we should diversify our investments, because when they are all in one sector and that sector has a bad year, we may suffer great losses.

Lastly, in chapter seven, we learned that we can change our day-to-day spending to avoid unnecessary purchases. By employing this tactic, we can free up more money to invest in Assets.

We also discussed financial freedom and passive Income. We saw that many people live their lives free from the need to work. With passive Income, people put their money to work for them. They use their money to make more money. Once you reach the point where the money that comes in from your investments is enough to pay for your living expenses, you will no longer be obligated to work.

My biggest motivation to write this book and to start investing, was the idea of financial freedom. We are raised to think that we need to get a good job to be happy, but in an ideal world, you may not even want to work. You may want more time to spend with your family or travel. There is nothing wrong with that. You just need to achieve a financial position that allows you to live that lifestyle.

❉ ❉ ❉

I hope this book has changed the way you think about money. I want you to actively think about how your money is being allocated. This is not a book about greed. It is about securing a financial position that you are comfortable with. It is about introducing you to ideas which with you may not be familiar.

After reading this book, you are now on the path to begin your own journey toward financial freedom.

I hope to meet you there.

ABOUT THE AUTHOR

Shlomo Bar-Eli

Shlomo grew up in Brooklyn, NY. After graduating from CUNY Brooklyn College with a degree in accounting, he went on to learn more about finance, investing, and real estate.

His goal is to raise awareness and help ordinary people become familiar with basic financial concepts to help guide them through the complicated world of money.

By changing how we think about our spending, and employing these simple strategies, he believes ANY person can improve their financial situation.

www.ingramcontent.com/pod-product-compliance
Lightning Source LLC
Chambersburg PA
CBHW030503220526
45464CB00006B/2640